DRUNK ENOUGH TO SAY I LOVE YOU?

by **Caryl Churchill**

Sam **Ty Burrell**
Jack **Stephen Dillane**

Director **James Macdonald**
Designer **Eugene Lee**
Costume Designer **Joan Wadge**
Lighting Designer **Peter Mumford**
Sound Designer **Ian Dickinson**
Composer **Matthew Herbert**
Assistant Director **Lyndsey Turner**
Casting **Lisa Makin**
US Casting **Heidi Griffiths, Jordan Thaler**
Production Manager **Paul Handley**
Stage Manager **Tariq Sayyid Rifaat**
Deputy Stage Manager **Emma Cameron**
Assistant Stage Manager **Patrick Birch**
Costume Supervisor **Jackie Orton**
Set built by **Rupert Blakeley**
Set painted by **Charlotte Gainey**

Ty Burrell is appearing with the permission of Actors' Equity Association
pursuant to an exchange program between American Equity and UK Equity.

THE COMPANY

Caryl Churchill (writer)
For the Royal Court: Owners, Light Shining in Buckinghamshire (Joint Stock), Cloud Nine (Joint Stock), Top Girls, Fen (Joint Stock), Serious Money, Ice Cream, Mad Forest (Central School of Speech and Drama), Thyestes (translation from Seneca), This is a Chair, Blue Heart (Out of Joint), Far Away, A Number.
Other theatre includes: Vinegar Tom (Monstrous Regiment); Softcops (RSC); The Skriker (National); Lives of the Great Poisoners, Hotel (Second Stride); A Dream Play (version from Strindberg, National).

Ty Burrell
Theatre includes: Macbeth (Broadway); Show People (Second Stage, New York); Burn This (Signature Theatre Co., New York); Richard III (Public, New York); Corners, The Blue Demon (Williamstown Theatre Festival); Cloud Nine, Babble (Broad Horizons Theatre Co., New York); Fool for Love (English-American Theatre Festival); King John, Twelfth Night, Coriolanus (The Shakespeare Theatre); The Lion in Winter, A Midsummer Night's Dream, Henry V (Utah Shakespearean Festival).
Television includes: Out of Practice, Law and Order, Law and Order: SVU, The West Wing, Lipshitz Saves the World.
Film includes: Fur, Friends with Money, Darwin Awards, In Good Company, Down in the Valley, Dawn of the Dead, Black Hawk Down, Evolution.

Stephen Dillane
For the Royal Court: Our Late Night, Hush. Other theatre includes: Macbeth (Los Angeles/Almeida); Coast of Utopia, Angels in America, A Long Day's Journey into Night, Dancing at Lughnasa (National); The Real Thing (Donmar/Albery/Broadway); Uncle Vanya (Young Vic/RSC); Hurlyburly (Old Vic); Endgame (Donmar); Hamlet (Gielgud).
Television includes: The Cazalets, Anna Karenina, Kings in Grass Castles, The Widowing of Mrs Holroyd, The Rector's Wife, Heading Home, Christabel.
Film includes: Savage Grace, Fugitive Pieces,

Goal!, Klimt, The Greatest Game Ever Played, Nine Lives, Haven, King Arthur, The Hours, Spy Game, The Parole Officer, Ordinary Decent Criminal, The Darkest Light, Welcome to Sarajevo, Firelight, Hamlet. Radio includes: Month in the Country, Oates after His Fingers, The Bayeux Tapestry, First Love, The Art of Love.

Ian Dickinson (sound designer)
For the Royal Court: Krapp's Last Tape, Piano/Forte, Rock 'n' Roll (& Duke of York's), Motortown, Rainbow Kiss, The Winterling, Alice Trilogy, Fewer Emergencies, Way to Heaven, The Woman Before, Stoning Mary (& Drum Theatre, Plymouth), Breathing Corpses, Wild East, Dumb Show, Shining City (& Gate, Dublin), Lucky Dog, Blest Be the Tie (with Talawa), Ladybird, Notes on Falling Leaves, Loyal Women, The Sugar Syndrome, Blood, Playing the Victim (with Told By an Idiot), Fallout, Flesh Wound, Hitchcock Blonde (& Lyric), Black Milk, Crazyblackmuthafuckin'self, Caryl Churchill Shorts, Push Up, Fucking Games, Herons.
Other theatre includes: Pillars of the Community (National); A Few Good Men (Haymarket); Port, As You Like It, Poor Superman, Martin Yesterday, Fast Food, Coyote Ugly (Royal Exchange, Manchester); Night of the Soul (RSC/Barbican); Eyes of the Kappa (Gate); Crime & Punishment in Dalston (Arcola); Search & Destroy (New End); The Whore's Dream (RSC/Edinburgh). Ian is Head of Sound at the Royal Court.

Matthew Herbert (composer)
Matthew is a classically trained pianist, but is better known for his work in the electronic music scene. He records under his own name as well as Doctor Rockit, Wishmountain, Radio Boy and others. He has also produced and remixed artists as diverse as Björk, REM, John Cale, Roisin Murphy, Yoko Ono and Serge Gainsbourg.
Albums include: Around the House, Bodily Functions, Goodbye Swingtime, Plat du Jour, Scale.

Eugene Lee (designer)
Theatre includes: A Number (New York); Wicked (Broadway/West End); Sweeney Todd, Agnes of God, Moon for the Misbegotten, Showboat, Ragtime (Broadway); Slaveship, Alice in Wonderland, Normal Heart, Vanya on 42nd Street, Grandchild of Kings, Ruby Sunrise (Off Broadway). Television includes: Saturday Night Live. Awards include: Tony Award, The American Theatre Wing's Design Award, The Outer Critics' Circle Award, The Drama Desk Award, The Pell Award, The Lucille Lortel Award.

James Macdonald (director)
For the Royal Court: Dying City, Fewer Emergencies, Lucky Dog, Blood, Blasted, 4.48 Psychosis, Hard Fruit, Real Classy Affair, Cleansed, Bailegangaire, Harry and Me, The Changing Room, Simpatico, Blasted, Peaches, Thyestes, The Terrible Voice of Satan, Hammett's Apprentice, Putting Two and Two Together.
Other theatre includes: Exiles (National); A Number (New York Theatre Workshop); Troilus und Cressida, Die Kopien (Berlin Schaubühne); 4.48 Psychose (Vienna Burgtheater); The Tempest, Roberto Zucco (RSC); The Triumph of Love (Almeida); Love's Labour's Lost, Richard II (Royal Exchange, Manchester); The Rivals (Nottingham Playhouse); The Crackwalker (Gate); The Seagull (Sheffield Crucible); Miss Julie (Oldham Coliseum); Juno and the Paycock, Ice Cream and Hot Fudge, Romeo and Juliet, Fool for Love, Savage/Love, Master Harold and the Boys (Contact Theatre); Prem (BAC/Soho Poly).
Opera includes: Eugene Onegin, Rigoletto (WNO); Die Zauberflöte (Garsington); Wolf Club Village, Night Banquet (Almeida Opera); Oedipus Rex, Survivor from Warsaw (Royal Exchange/Hallé); Lives of the Great Poisoners (Second Stride).
James has been Associate Director of the Royal Court since 1992.

Peter Mumford (lighting designer)
For the Royal Court: Dying City (& set design), Blood.
Other theatre includes: Waiting for Godot (New Ambassador's); Voyage Round My Father (Donmar/Wyndham's); Summer and Smoke (Apollo); Exiles (National); Amy's View (Garrick); Richard II (Old Vic); two seasons of work for the Peter Hall Company, including Much Ado About Nothing (Theatre Royal, Bath); Hedda Gabler, The Goat (Almeida/West End); The Far Pavilions (Shaftesbury); The King and I (UK tour); The Playboy of the Western World (Abbey Theatre/US tour); Blithe Spirit (Savoy); Out of this World, The Master and Margarita, A Midsummer Night's Dream, Three Women and a Piano Tuner (Chichester Festival); Becket (Theatre Royal, Haymarket); Brand, Macbeth (RSC/West End); Vincent in Brixton (National/West End/New York); Private Lives (West End/Broadway); Hamlet (RSC/Barbican); Bacchai (National/Epidavros amphitheatre); The Talking Cure, Luther and Summerfolk, Merchant of Venice (National); Cinderella, The Nutcracker (Scottish Ballet). Opera includes: Madame Butterfly (ENO/The Met); The Coronation of Poppea, Falstaff (ENO); La Cenerentola (Glyndebourne); Fidelio (Scottish Opera); Passion (Minnesota Opera); Cosi Fan Tutte (ENO/Barbican); Il Trovatore (Paris); La Traviata (Antwerp); Siegfried Götterdämmerung (Scottish Opera/Edinburgh Festival); Eugene Onegin, Madama Butterfly (Opera North); Giulio Cesare (Bordeaux); Eugine Onegin, The Bartered Bride (Royal Opera House/Helsinki).
Awards include: The 2003 Olivier Award for Best Lighting Design for The Bacchae; the 1995 Olivier Award for Outstanding Achievement in Dance for The Glass Blew In and Fearful Symmetries (Royal Ballet).

Lyndsey Turner (assistant director)
As assistant director for the Royal Court:
Krapp's Last Tape, The Winterling.
As director theatre includes: Contractions,
Still Breathing, What's Their Life Got, Paris
Hilton, The Good Guy Gets the Girl, Hymn
(Theatre 503); Halo Boy and the Village of
Death (Edinburgh Fringe Festival); Antony
and Cleopatra, Twelve Angry Men, Arabian
Nights, The Servant to Two Masters (MFH).
As assistant director theatre includes: The
Love of the Nightingale (RADA).
Lyndsey is currently the Royal Court's
Trainee Director.

Joan Wadge (costume designer)
For the Royal Court: A Number, Plasticine.
Other theatre includes: Tintin (Barbican);
Festen (Almeida/West End); Afore Night
Come (Young Vic); Albert Speer (National)
Opera includes: The Love Potion (Pegasus
Opera Co.).
Film and television includes: Under the
Greenwood Tree, Adventures of the Worst
Witch, Heaven on Earth, The Phoenix and
the Carpet, The Lenny Henry Show, Ivanhoe,
Henry IV, The Great Kandinsky, The House of
Eliott – Series 1 & 3, The Adventures of
Christopher Columbus, In Dreams, Old
Times, Antonia and Jane – A Definitive
Annual Report, Summer's Lease, All Passion
Spent, The Interrogation of John.
Awards include: EMMY Award for Costume
Design for House of Eliott 1994; BAFTA for
Costume Design for House of Eliott 1993.

THE ENGLISH STAGE COMPANY AT THE ROYAL COURT

The English Stage Company at the Royal Court opened in 1956 as a subsidised theatre producing new British plays, international plays and some classical revivals.

The first artistic director George Devine aimed to create a writers' theatre, 'a place where the dramatist is acknowledged as the fundamental creative force in the theatre and where the play is more important than the actors, the director, the designer'. The urgent need was to find a contemporary style in which the play, the acting, direction and design are all combined. He believed that 'the battle will be a long one to continue to create the right conditions for writers to work in'.

Devine aimed to discover 'hard-hitting, uncompromising writers whose plays are stimulating, provocative and exciting'. The Royal Court production of John Osborne's Look Back in Anger in May 1956 is now seen as the decisive starting point of modern British drama and the policy created a new generation of British playwrights. The first wave included John Osborne, Arnold Wesker, John Arden, Ann Jellicoe, N F Simpson and Edward Bond. Early seasons included new international plays by Bertolt Brecht, Eugène Ionesco, Samuel Beckett and Jean-Paul Sartre.

The theatre started with the 400-seat proscenium arch Theatre Downstairs, and in 1969 opened a second theatre, the 60-seat studio Theatre Upstairs. Some productions transfer to the West End, such as Tom Stoppard's Rock 'n' Roll, My Name is Rachel Corrie, Terry Johnson's Hitchcock Blonde, Caryl Churchill's Far Away and Conor McPherson's The Weir. Recent touring productions include Sarah Kane's 4.48 Psychosis (US tour) and Ché Walker's Flesh Wound (Galway Arts Festival). The Royal Court also co-produces plays which transfer to the West End or tour internationally, such as Conor McPherson's Shining City (with Gate Theatre, Dublin), Sebastian Barry's The Steward of Christendom and Mark Ravenhill's Shopping and Fucking (with Out of Joint), Martin McDonagh's The Beauty Queen Of Leenane (with Druid), Ayub Khan Din's East is East (with Tamasha).

Since 1994 the Royal Court's artistic policy has again been vigorously directed to finding and producing a new generation of playwrights. The writers include Joe Penhall, Rebecca Prichard, Michael Wynne, Nick Grosso, Judy Upton, Meredith Oakes, Sarah Kane, Anthony Neilson, Judith Johnson, James Stock, Jez Butterworth,

photo: Stephen Cummiiskey

Marina Carr, Phyllis Nagy, Simon Block, Martin McDonagh, Mark Ravenhill, Ayub Khan Din, Tamantha Hammerschlag, Jess Walters, Ché Walker, Conor McPherson, Simon Stephens, Richard Bean, Roy Williams, Gary Mitchell, Mick Mahoney, Rebecca Gilman, Christopher Shinn, Kia Corthron, David Gieselmann, Marius von Mayenburg, David Eldridge, Leo Butler, Zinnie Harris, Grae Cleugh, Roland Schimmelpfennig, Chloe Moss, DeObia Oparei, Enda Walsh, Vassily Sigarev, the Presnyakov Brothers, Marcos Barbosa, Lucy Prebble, John Donnelly, Clare Pollard, Robin French, Elyzabeth Gregory Wilder, Rob Evans, Laura Wade, Debbie Tucker Green, Levi David Addai and Simon Farquhar. This expanded programme of new plays has been made possible through the support of A.S.K. Theater Projects and the Skirball Foundation, The Jerwood Charity, the American Friends of the Royal Court Theatre and (in 1994/5 and 1999) the National Theatre Studio.

The refurbished theatre in Sloane Square opened in February 2000, with a policy still inspired by the first artistic director George Devine. The Royal Court is an international theatre for new plays and new playwrights, and the work shapes contemporary drama in Britain and overseas.

The Royal Court's long and successful history of innovation has been built by generations of gifted and imaginative individuals. In 2006, the company celebrates its 50th Anniversary, an important landmark for the performing arts in Britain. For information on the many exciting ways you can help support the theatre, please contact the Development Department on 020 7565 5079.

AWARDS FOR
THE ROYAL COURT

Martin McDonagh won the 1996 George Devine Award, the 1996 Writers' Guild Best Fringe Play Award, the 1996 Critics' Circle Award and the 1996 Evening Standard Award for Most Promising Playwright for The Beauty Queen of Leenane. Marina Carr won the 19th Susan Smith Blackburn Prize (1996/7) for Portia Coughlan. Conor McPherson won the 1997 George Devine Award, the 1997 Critics' Circle Award and the 1997 Evening Standard Award for Most Promising Playwright for The Weir. Ayub Khan Din won the 1997 Writers' Guild Awards for Best West End Play and New Writer of the Year and the 1996 John Whiting Award for East is East (co-production with Tamasha).

Martin McDonagh's The Beauty Queen of Leenane (co-production with Druid Theatre Company) won four 1998 Tony Awards including Garry Hynes for Best Director. Eugene Ionesco's The Chairs (co-production with Theatre de Complicite) was nominated for six Tony awards. David Hare won the 1998 Time Out Live Award for Outstanding Achievement and six awards in New York including the Drama League, Drama Desk and New York Critics Circle Award for Via Dolorosa. Sarah Kane won the 1998 Arts Foundation Fellowship in Playwriting. Rebecca Prichard won the 1998 Critics' Circle Award for Most Promising Playwright for Yard Gal (co-production with Clean Break).

Conor McPherson won the 1999 Olivier Award for Best New Play for The Weir. The Royal Court won the 1999 ITI Award for Excellence in International Theatre. Sarah Kane's Cleansed was judged Best Foreign Language Play in 1999 by Theater Heute in Germany. Gary Mitchell won the 1999 Pearson Best Play Award for Trust. Rebecca Gilman was joint winner of the 1999 George Devine Award and won the 1999 Evening Standard Award for Most Promising Playwright for The Glory of Living.

In 1999, the Royal Court won the European theatre prize New Theatrical Realities, presented at Taormina Arte in Sicily, for its efforts in recent years in discovering and producing the work of young British dramatists.

Roy Williams and Gary Mitchell were joint winners of the George Devine Award 2000 for Most Promising Playwright for Lift Off and The Force of Change respectively. At the Barclays Theatre Awards 2000 presented by the TMA, Richard Wilson won the Best Director Award for David Gieselmann's Mr Kolpert and Jeremy Herbert won the Best Designer Award for Sarah Kane's 4.48 Psychosis. Gary Mitchell won the Evening Standard's Charles Wintour Award 2000 for Most Promising Playwright for The Force of Change. Stephen Jeffreys' I Just Stopped by to See the Man won an AT&T: On Stage Award 2000.

David Eldridge's Under the Blue Sky won the Time Out Live Award 2001 for Best New Play in the West End. Leo Butler won the George Devine Award 2001 for Most Promising Playwright for Redundant. Roy Williams won the Evening Standard's Charles Wintour Award 2001 for Most Promising Playwright for Clubland. Grae Cleugh won the 2001 Olivier Award for Most Promising Playwright for Fucking Games.

Richard Bean was joint winner of the George Devine Award 2002 for Most Promising Playwright for Under the Whaleback. Caryl Churchill won the 2002 Evening Standard Award for Best New Play for A Number. Vassily Sigarev won the 2002 Evening Standard Charles Wintour Award for Most Promising Playwright for Plasticine. Ian MacNeil won the 2002 Evening Standard Award for Best Design for A Number and Plasticine. Peter Gill won the 2002 Critics' Circle Award for Best New Play for The York Realist (English Touring Theatre). Ché Walker won the 2003 George Devine Award for Most Promising Playwright for Flesh Wound. Lucy Prebble won the 2003 Critics' Circle Award and the 2004 George Devine Award for Most Promising Playwright, and the TMA Theatre Award 2004 for Best New Play for The Sugar Syndrome.

Richard Bean won the 2005 Critics' Circle Award for Best New Play for Harvest. Laura Wade won the 2005 Critics' Circle Award for Most Promising Playwright and the 2005 Pearson Best Play Award for Breathing Corpses. The 2006 Whatsonstage Theatregoers' Choice Award for Best New Play was won by My Name is Rachel Corrie.

The 2005 Evening Standard Special Award was given to the Royal Court 'for making and changing theatrical history this last half century'.

ROYAL COURT BOOKSHOP

The Royal Court bookshop offers a range of contemporary plays and publications on the theory and practice of modern drama. The staff specialise in assisting with the selection of audition monologues and scenes.Royal Court playtexts from past and present productions cost £2.

The Bookshop is situated just above the ROYAL COURT CAFE BAR.

Monday–Friday 3–10pm

Saturday 2.30–10pm

For information tel: 020 7565 5024

or email: bookshop@royalcourttheatre.com

PROGRAMME SUPPORTERS

The Royal Court (English Stage Company Ltd) receives its principal funding from Arts Council England, London. It is also supported financially by a wide range of private companies, charitable and public bodies, and earns the remainder of its income from the box office and its own trading activities.

The Genesis Foundation supports the Royal Court's work with International Playwrights.

Archival recordings of the Royal Court's Anniversary year are made possible by Francis Finlay.

The Skirball Foundation funds a Playwrights' Programme at the theatre. The Artistic Director's Chair is supported by a lead grant from The Peter Jay Sharp Foundation, contributing to the activities of the Artistic Director's office. Over the past nine years the BBC has supported the Gerald Chapman Fund for directors.

The Jerwood Charity supports new plays by new playwrights through the Jerwood New Playwrights series.

ROYAL COURT
DEVELOPMENT BOARD
Tamara Ingram (Chair)
Jonathan Cameron
(Vice Chair)
Timothy Burrill
Anthony Burton
Jonathan Caplan QC
Sindy Caplan
Gavin Casey FCA
Mark Crowdy
Cas Donald
Celeste Fenichel
Joseph Fiennes
Amanda Foreman
Gavin Neath
Michael Potter
Kadee Robbins
Mark Robinson
William Russell
James L Tanner

PUBLIC FUNDING
Arts Council England,
London
British Council
London Challenge
Royal Borough of
Kensington & Chelsea

TRUSTS AND
FOUNDATIONS
The ADAPT Trust
American Friends of the
Royal Court Theatre
Gerald Chapman Fund
Columbia Foundation
The Sidney & Elizabeth
Corob Charitable Trust
Cowley Charitable Trust
The Dorset Foundation
The Ronald Duncan
Literary Foundation
Earls Court and Olympia
Charitable Trust
The Foyle Foundation
Francis Finlay
The Garfield Weston
Foundation
Genesis Foundation
Jerwood Charity
Lloyds TSB Foundation for
England and Wales
Lynn Foundation
John Lyon's Charity
The Magowan Family
Foundation

The Laura Pels Foundation
The Peggy Ramsay
Foundation
The Rayne Foundation
Rose Foundation
The Royal Victoria Hall
Foundation
The Peter Jay Sharp
Foundation
Skirball Foundation
Wates Foundation
Michael J Zamkow &
Sue E Berman Charitable
Trust

50TH ANNIVERSARY
PROGRAMME SPONSOR
Coutts & Co

SPONSORS
Aviva Plc
BBC
Cadogan Hotel
City Inn
Dom Pérignon
Doughty Street Chambers
dunhill
Giorgio Armani
Links of London
John Malkovich/Uncle
Kimono
Pemberton Greenish
Simons Muirhead & Burton
Smythson of Bond Street
Vanity Fair
White Light

CORPORATE
BENEFACTORS
Insinger de Beaufort
Merrill Lynch

BUSINESS AND MEDIA
MEMBERS
AKA
Bloomsbury
Columbia Tristar Films
(UK)
Digby Trout Restaurants
Grey London
The Henley Centre
Lazard
Peter Jones
Slaughter and May

PRODUCTION SYNDICATE
Anonymous
Dianne & Michael Bienes
Ms Kay Ellen Consolver
Mrs Philip Donald
John Garfield
Peter & Edna Goldstein
Daisy Prince
Kadee Robbins
William & Hilary Russell
Kay Hartenstein Saatchi
Jon & NoraLee Sedmak
Ian & Carol Sellars

INDIVIDUAL MEMBERS
Patrons
Anonymous
Dr Bettina Bahlsen
Katie Bradford
Marcus J Burton & Dr M F
Ozbilgin
Mr & Mrs Philip Donald
Tom & Simone Fenton
Daniel & Joanna Friel
John Garfield
Lady Grabiner
Charles & Elizabeth Handy
Jan Harris
Jack & Linda Keenan
Pawel & Sarah Kisielewski
Deborah & Stephen
Marquardt
Duncan Matthews QC
Jill & Paul Ruddock
Ian & Carol Sellars
Jan & Michael Topham
Richard Wilson OBE

Benefactors
Anonymous
Martha Allfrey
Amanda Attard-Manché
Varian Ayers & Gary
Knisely
John & Anoushka Ayton
Mr & Mrs Gavin Casey
Sindy & Jonathan Caplan
Jeremy Conway & Nicola
Van Gelder
Robyn Durie
Hugo Eddis
Joachim Fleury
Beverley Gee
Sue and Don Guiney
Claire Guinness
Sam & Caroline Haubold
Tamara Ingram

David Juxon
David Kaskell &
Christopher Teano
Peter & Maria Kellner
Larry & Peggy Levy
Barbara Minto
Mr & Mrs Richard Pilosof
Elaine Potter
Anthony Simpson
Brian D Smith
Sue Stapely
Sir Robert & Lady Wilson
Nick Wheeler
Sir Mark & Lady Wrightson

Associates
Act IV
Anonymous
Jeffrey Archer
Brian Boylan
Alan Brodie
Ossi & Paul Burger
Clive & Helena Butler
Gaynor Buxton
Lady Cazalet
Carole & Neville Conrad
Margaret Cowper
Andrew Cryer
Linda & Ronald F. Daitz
Zoë Dominic
Kim Dunn
Celeste Fenichel
Charlotte & Nick Fraser
Gillian Frumkin
Sara Galbraith
Jacqueline & Jonathan
Gestetner
Vivien Goodwin
David & Suzie Hyman
Mrs Ellen Josefowitz
Colette & Peter Levy
Mr Watcyn Lewis
David Marks
Nicola McFarland
Gavin & Ann Neath
Janet & Michael Orr
S. Osman
Pauline Pinder
William Poeton CBE &
Barbara Poeton
Jeremy Priestley
Beverley Rider
John Ritchie
Lois Sieff OBE
Gail Steele
Will Turner
Anthony Wigram

FOR THE ROYAL COURT

Royal Court Theatre, Sloane Square, London SW1W 8AS
Tel: 020 7565 5050 Fax: 020 7565 5001
info@royalcourttheatre.com
www.royalcourttheatre.com

Artistic Director **Ian Rickson**
Associate Director International **Elyse Dodgson**
Associate Director **Ramin Gray**
Associate Director Casting **Lisa Makin**
Associate Director (50th) **Emily McLaughlin+**
Associate Directors* **James Macdonald,
Max Stafford-Clark, Richard Wilson**
Literary Manager **Graham Whybrow**
Literary Associate **Terry Johnson***
Casting Deputy **Amy Ball**
International Associate **Orla O'Loughlin**
International Administrator **Chris James**
Trainee Director **Lyndsey Turner**
Artistic Assistant **Rebecca Hanna-Grindall**

Production Manager **Paul Handley**
Deputy Production Manager **Sue Bird**
Production Assistant **Sarah Davies**
Head of Lighting **Johanna Town**
Lighting Deputy **Greg Gould**
Lighting Assistants **Nicki Brown, Kelli Marston**
Lighting Board Operator **Stephen Andrews**
Head of Stage **Steven Stickler**
Stage Deputy **Daniel Lockett**
Stage Chargehand **Lee Crimmen**
Head of Sound **Ian Dickinson**
Sound Deputy **Emma Laxton**
Acting Head of Costume **Laura Hunt**
Costume Deputy **Jackie Orton**

YOUNG WRITERS PROGRAMME
Associate Director **Ola Animashawun**
Administrator **Nina Lyndon**
Administrator (Maternity Cover) **Claire Birch**
Outreach Worker **Lucy Dunkerley**
Education Officer **Laura McCluskey***
Writers' Tutor **Leo Butler***

General Manager **Diane Borger**
Administrator **Oliver Rance**
Finance Director **Sarah Preece**
Finance Officer **Rachel Harrison***
Finance Officer **Martin Wheeler**
Finance Manager **Helen Perryer***

Head of Press **Ewan Thomson**
Press Associate **Tamsin Treverton Jones***
Press Assistant **Steve Pidcock**
Press Intern **Amanda Dekker**

Marketing Consultant **Kym Bartlett***
Advertising and Marketing Agency **aka**
Marketing Assistant **Gemma Frayne**
Marketing Intern **Áine Mulkeen**
Sales Manager **David Kantounas**
Deputy Sales Manager **Stuart Grey**
Box Office Sales Assistants **Helen Bennett,
Maria Ferran, Samantha Preston**

Head of Development **Nicky Jones**
Development Manager **Leona Felton**
Trusts and Foundations Manager **Gaby Styles**
Sponsorship Officer **Natalie Moss**
Development Intern **Rebecca Bond**

Theatre Manager **Bobbie Stokes**
Front of House Managers **Nathalie Meghriche,
Lucinda Springett**
Bar and Food Manager **Darren Elliott**
Deputy Bar and Food Manager **Claire Simpson**
Duty House Managers **Charlie Revell*, Matt Wood***
Bookshop Manager **Simon David**
Assistant Bookshop Manager **Edin Suljic***
Bookshop Assistants **Nicki Welburn*, Fiona Clift***
Stage Door/Reception **Simon David*, Jon Hunter,
Paul Lovegrove, Tyrone Lucas**

Thanks to all of our box office assistants, ushers
and bar staff.

+ The Associate Director post is supported by the BBC
through the Gerald Chapman Fund.

* Part-time.

DRUNK ENOUGH TO SAY I LOVE YOU?

Caryl Churchill

Characters

JACK

SAM

1.

JACK	drunk enough to say I love you?
SAM	never say
JACK	not that I don't still love my wife and children but
SAM	who doesn't want to be loved? but
JACK	first time I saw you
SAM	the bar and the guy with
JACK	never see you again and I was fine with that, I thought one night and I'll love him till I die but that's ok, I can live
SAM	you know something?
JACK	and then I'm here and suddenly here you are and here we are again and
SAM	because I'm leaving tomorrow so
JACK	sorry of course but just as well because
SAM	and you could come with me if you
JACK	I
SAM	if you want
JACK	of course I

SAM   so you'll

JACK   so no I can't possibly

SAM   of course not

JACK   no

SAM   glad you came up and said hi because
           when you reminded me it all came back
           though to be honest I'd forgotten till you

JACK   can't say no oh god can't let you

SAM   so you'll

JACK   what I'm going to tell them. How long

SAM   as long as it

JACK   family obviously but work, I'm in the
           middle

SAM   sure you'll figure it out, I don't need to

JACK   go where did you say you?

SAM   anywhere you wouldn't?

JACK   do when we get there?

SAM   things you won't do?

2.

SAM	elections
JACK	how to win
SAM	because democracy
JACK	help the right side to
SAM	because our security
JACK	all over the world
SAM	Vietnam we have the slogan 'Christ has gone south' so the people think
JACK	Christians because of the French
SAM	literally believe literally Jesus Christ has
JACK	so clever
SAM	and simultaneously astrology
JACK	superstitious
SAM	horoscopes daily horoscopes will say
JACK	and they vote the way you want, that is so
SAM	because you have to appeal to their deepest
JACK	I love this
SAM	and Chile, this is good, we put it on the radio 'your children taken from you', if

	they vote communist they lose their children, the Russians will take
JACK	appealing to the women's vote
SAM	so the pamphlets must say 'privately printed by citizens with no political affiliations' because
JACK	big budget
SAM	and syndicate the articles all over the world
JACK	so nobody
SAM	and posters
JACK	great artwork
SAM	with the hammer and sickle stamped on their foreheads
JACK	little kids
SAM	hammer and sickle
JACK	love a copy of that to put
SAM	So help me out here, in Nicaragua we need to be telling different things to different groups, say
JACK	fighting to keep the Russians off their land because peasants
SAM	while the workers
JACK	that they'll lose their factories
SAM	doctors

JACK	replaced by Cubans
SAM	way to go.
JACK	so happy, you, the work, the whole
SAM	polls in the Phillipines?
JACK	so I'll make the numbers up
SAM	good at this
JACK	thrilling.
SAM	don't always work out the way we
JACK	voting for the wrong
SAM	Chavez
JACK	how did
SAM	Hamas
JACK	Israelis arresting the MPs so
SAM	so now we need to prevent some elections
JACK	saves having to overthrow
SAM	South Korea, Guatemala, Brazil, Congo, Indonesia, Greece
JACK	I'm on it
SAM	overthrow only as last resort when things don't
JACK	ok
SAM	Iran Guatemala Iraq Congo
JACK	troops.

SAM	coffee
JACK	two sugars
SAM	invading Grenada to get rid of the government because
JACK	byebye Lumumba
SAM	byebye Allende
JACK	bit negative
SAM	people we love and help
JACK	always love Israel
SAM	shah of Iran, byebye Mossadegh
JACK	oil
SAM	warlords in Afghanistan, Hekmatya
JACK	drives over people?
SAM	acid
JACK	ok
SAM	don't like that government in Afghanistan because the Russians like it so we're tricking them into invading
JACK	oops
SAM	puts them in the wrong plus it's their Vietnam so get on now with training the mujahadeen which is freedom fighters to
JACK	whooo
SAM	haha

JACK	so we're helping all these
SAM	kind of want to help Pol Pot because
JACK	killing fields guy?
SAM	against Vietnam but no we can't be seen to directly support someone who
JACK	so why don't we help China help him
SAM	knew I was right to bring you
JACK	because no one can blame us for what the Chinese
SAM	get people to do things for you like Saddam Hussein
JACK	great
SAM	shake his hand
JACK	holding down the Iranians
SAM	great job
JACK	lot of dead in that one
SAM	and all costs money
JACK	to help the elections turn out
SAM	plus training their police, their armies
JACK	so much aid
SAM	and two hundred and fifty million dollars to the Philippines alone to train fifty thousand soldiers
JACK	plus military advisers

SAM   remember to use green berets of Puerto
               Rican and Mexican descent so it won't
               look like a US army because

JACK   ha

SAM   would you believe six billion dollars in El
               Salvador? training thousands of

JACK   and the schools, I'm trying to organise

SAM   School of the Americas

JACK   coup school

SAM   chemical school

JACK   enormous

SAM   results in and we won in

JACK   yay

SAM   and we've got our man in Afghanistan

JACK   cia guy?

SAM   Georgia, check

JACK   Uzbekistan? because they boil

SAM   not so good in Bolivia

JACK   guy in the sweater?

SAM   and Saddam's let us down, he's no longer
               a good guy so

JACK   because sometimes propaganda isn't
               enough to

SAM   military solution

JACK   so much fun in my life

SAM   being powerful and being on the side of
              good is

JACK   god must have so much fun

SAM   win win win

JACK   love you more than I can

3.

SAM	sitting around
JACK	not
SAM	so much to do because
JACK	thinking
SAM	no time for
JACK	all right I'm just
SAM	missing your
JACK	not at all
SAM	natural
JACK	get on with
SAM	because there's all these people we have to
JACK	ok so here's the bridge right here and the people there are people going across not soldiers just
SAM	Korea
JACK	blow it up
SAM	there you go
JACK	don't want you to worry because I don't regret

SAM	death squads
JACK	right behind
SAM	in Guatemala, so we don't directly ourselves appear to
JACK	corpses in the nets
SAM	decapitated, castrated, eyes gouged out, testicles
JACK	riddled with bullets and partially eaten by fish
SAM	slaughter the indians to prevent
JACK	bulldoze the village
SAM	yes
JACK	and
SAM	not officially active in El Salvador
JACK	seventy-five thousand civilian
SAM	raping the
JACK	because if the young aren't killed they just grow up to be
SAM	similarly Colombia where
JACK	Nicaragua
SAM	our freedom fighters the Contras are
JACK	Indonesia the US embassy are giving lists to the army which are a big help in who they should

SAM   mass slaying

JACK   there you are

SAM   and of course Israel where we don't
            actually ourselves

JACK   extremely valuable experiment in the
            Philippines where

SAM   calling it search and destroy

JACK   experiments in pacification

SAM   terror against the Huks

JACK   and applying that now in Vietnam

SAM   Vietnam Vietnam now

JACK   go go go three million dead in Vietnam
            Laos Cambodia

SAM   two million tons of bombs on Laos now

JACK   more than on Germany and Japan in the
            whole

SAM   white phosphorus

JACK   statistics here on civilian injuries, lower
            extremities 60 per cent, soft tissue 39 per
            cent, fractures

SAM   not that interested

JACK   Iraq

SAM   not that interested in numbers of civilian

JACK   no

SAM   need to get on

JACK   I'm on it

SAM   Iraq

JACK   hundred and seventyseven million pounds
              of

SAM   forty days

JACK   ten thousand sorties

SAM   very few casualties

JACK   oh ours, good

SAM   bombing them now as they retreat

JACK   ploughing wow ploughing live soldiers into
              the sand

SAM   done

JACK   and the children dead from sanctions we
              don't count that because

SAM   again Iraq Iraq again

JACK   very few casualties

SAM   not publishing pictures

JACK   and certainly not of the civilians in
              Afghanistan there's a paper in Florida
              making a mistake there getting a lot of
              emails and won't do that again

SAM   bombing Vietnam now, bombing
              Grenada, bombing Korea, bombing Laos,
              bombing Guatemala, bombing Cuba,
              bombing El Salvador, bombing Iraq,
              bombing Somalia, bombing Lebanon

JACK	but it's Israel bombing
SAM	so? bombing Bosnia, bombing Cambodia, bombing Libya, bombing
JACK	used to be a village and now
SAM	because we want it gone
JACK	need a coffee
SAM	get a coffee
JACK	exhausting
SAM	thrilling
JACK	exhausting being so thrilled
SAM	coffee but keep
JACK	bombing China, bombing Panama
SAM	good at this
JACK	well
SAM	did a whole lot before like second world war and going right back
JACK	all the back killings before like indians
SAM	never sure how many we started
JACK	maybe twenty million, fifty
SAM	got them down to a quarter million so
JACK	not looking at that
SAM	no just get on with the job which is bombing
JACK	bombing Peru, bombing

4.

JACK	controlling
SAM	not
JACK	I feel
SAM	missing your family
JACK	only human, I'm naturally going to
SAM	just so I know where I am
JACK	expect me to just cut off everybody and not even speak
SAM	what you want
JACK	better if I do some work
SAM	drawing up trade agreements
JACK	free trade
SAM	in a manner of
JACK	free
SAM	structural adjustment programs
JACK	so that countries open up their markets to our
SAM	good ok like Haiti
JACK	surge in our rice exports to Haiti

SAM	ok
JACK	stopping the banana cartel
SAM	ok
JACK	and those beautiful African textiles made from our raw materials they agree to import rather than
SAM	or sometimes it's the other way, it's their raw materials like cocoa
JACK	and we make the chocolates you get on valentine's day
SAM	because if they were allowed to make them
JACK	and the rice industry collapses in Haiti
SAM	because our economy is the priority here
JACK	costing poor countries two billion dollars a day because
SAM	really snitty mood today
JACK	just trying to understand exactly
SAM	essential because we consume more than half the goods in the world so you can't
JACK	ok ok and privatisation a condition
SAM	because private means free
JACK	ok
SAM	problem with that?
JACK	just low today, I can't quite

SAM	better get a grip
JACK	ok so it's access for our goods
SAM	come on we've done debt cancellation here
JACK	yes I
SAM	and massive aid
JACK	linked to
SAM	what is the matter with you?
JACK	pointing out that it's 80% our own companies that benefit from
SAM	generosity
JACK	point one per cent of our
SAM	billions of dollars for christsake
JACK	just trying to see
SAM	yes and
JACK	Israel seems to get the largest share of
SAM	you want to go home?
JACK	didn't say
SAM	because if you don't want to be
JACK	I do
SAM	keep saying you love me and then we have all this
JACK	sorry
SAM	easy to

JACK	woke up feeling
SAM	maybe you should go back to bed and try again
JACK	no I'll be
SAM	you better be
JACK	ok.
SAM	something to make you feel better
JACK	don't really
SAM	good?
JACK	ah
SAM	french connection
JACK	mm?
SAM	golden triangle
JACK	sure
SAM	fighting communists for us so we turn a blind eye
JACK	of course
SAM	heroin being flown in by air america
JACK	excellent
SAM	flying down with the weapons and back with the drugs
JACK	shrimp company laundering the money so the cia

SAM	25 tons of cocaine though he himself is head of the antidrug
JACK	but also we are against
SAM	totally
JACK	like in Peru
SAM	supporting the dictator because he's fighting drugs
JACK	though I see here the cia payroll
SAM	because the main priority is suppressing the guerrillas
JACK	like in Colombia
SAM	because farc are definitely narcotraffickers
JACK	luckily
SAM	have to overlook the security services drug
JACK	and the equipment can also be used against political opponents which saves
SAM	and Afghanistan where of course the mujihadeen
JACK	beautiful fields of poppies
SAM	same trucks can deliver the arms and take the heroin back
JACK	simultaneously facilitate and crack down
SAM	massive trade figures
JACK	lot of people happy.

SAM	feeling better have a look at intellectual property rights
JACK	fascinating
SAM	forefront of science
JACK	traditional knowledge of primitive tribes which turns out to
SAM	neem
JACK	is what, neem?
SAM	in India
JACK	so we patent it do we and
SAM	ayehuasca, you ever heard ?
JACK	quinoa, kava, bitter gourd
SAM	so we're manufacturing products out of
JACK	and selling them back to
SAM	yes
JACK	and most amazingly dna
SAM	Amazonian Indian blood cells
JACK	the scale of it
SAM	per cent of human dna has been acquired by
JACK	my god how
SAM	so you're on that?
JACK	I'm on it.

SAM	because expenses are so great like eight billion dollars we spend on cosmetics
JACK	hard to grasp such
SAM	ten on petfood
JACK	for comparison
SAM	six on
JACK	enough to provide health, food and education for the whole of the third
SAM	fuck is wrong with you?
JACK	trying to grasp the numbers that's all, I
SAM	do things on a large scale
JACK	yes
SAM	way of life
JACK	yes
SAM	you chose
JACK	yes
SAM	can fuck off now if
JACK	no
SAM	yes fuck off now because
JACK	no please no
SAM	commitment

5.

SAM	space
JACK	god
SAM	all mine
JACK	so
SAM	deny others the use of space
JACK	it's just
SAM	we have it, we like it and we're going to keep it
JACK	fantastic
SAM	fight *in* space, we're going to fight *from* space, we're going to fight *into*
JACK	wow
SAM	you like it?
JACK	so big
SAM	star wars
JACK	and protect
SAM	protecting us with a shield
JACK	and nobody else can
SAM	precision strikes

JACK   though the UN

SAM   everyone else agrees a resolution not to
            use space so

JACK   giving us total

SAM   because with the proliferation of wmd

JACK   so many countries want

SAM   so we combat the threat by

JACK   I do worry about

SAM   because we have two and a half times the
            next nine countries put together

JACK   thank god

SAM   nuclear weapons stored in seven european

JACK   hey

SAM   chemical

JACK   whoo

SAM   go go go now dioxin

JACK   dioxin, god, three ounces in the water
            supply of New York would be enough to
            wipe out the whole

SAM   five hundred pounds dioxin now on
            Vietnam

JACK   yay

SAM   napalm

JACK   yay

SAM	sarin on Laos
JACK	yay
SAM	and biological too the most advanced
JACK	scientific
SAM	turkey feathers
JACK	feathers?
SAM	allegations by China that we
JACK	oh with germs on
SAM	decaying fish, anthrax
JACK	isn't it turkey in Cuba?
SAM	turkey virus in Cuba
JACK	ok
SAM	contaminate the sugar
JACK	quite funny
SAM	but the serious science
JACK	the chemical school in Alabama
SAM	teach our allies and share
JACK	Egypt's using gas against the Yemen, and Saddam's gassed the
SAM	exporting anthrax to Iraq, botulism, histoplasma capsulatum
JACK	e coli?
SAM	e coli, dna

JACK	this stuff against Kurds or Iranians or?
SAM	keep selling it because
JACK	so great about chemical and biological they don't destroy the buildings just kill the
SAM	ideal
JACK	and oh my god the conventional
SAM	cluster bombs
JACK	love the yellow
SAM	jagged steel shrapnel
JACK	soft targets
SAM	don't always explode like one and a half million unexploded in the gulf
JACK	very high rate of
SAM	no, out of thirty
JACK	ok
SAM	but sometimes a quarter
JACK	orange groves, car parks
SAM	so don't let Israel
JACK	ok
SAM	oh what the hell
JACK	ok
SAM	so you get these accidental
JACK	kids like the yellow

SAM   accidental loss of limbs

JACK   can't be helped

SAM   and the depleted uranium so you get the
             lung and bone cancer and

JACK   don't feel bad

SAM   babies, deformed

JACK   ugh

SAM   probably for other reasons

JACK   exactly

SAM   So, keeping ourselves safe

JACK   priority

SAM   bring freedom

JACK   love it when you say

SAM   most destructive power ever in the history
             of the

JACK   yes yes

SAM   and now space

JACK   stars

SAM   eternity filled with our

JACK   love you so

SAM   more and more

6.

SAM	faster
JACK	I'm
SAM	threat to our security
JACK	ok
SAM	if anyone harbours
JACK	I'm on it
SAM	retaliate against the facilities of the host country
JACK	yes
SAM	now
JACK	calm
SAM	got to plant bombs in the hotels in Havana
JACK	yes ok ok the Cuban exiles in Miami are just
SAM	and get the money to Iraq
JACK	done it, the Iraqi National Accord have the
SAM	and have they destabilised Saddam yet? no

JACK   car bombs

SAM   giving them millions

JACK   hundred civilians dead

SAM   not enough to

JACK   ok

SAM   fucking results

JACK   off my back will you?

SAM   desperate for

JACK   mujahadeen

SAM   yes yes train the

JACK   so ok that's something really good

SAM   stop at nothing, flaying, explosions, whole
            villages

JACK   and here we're getting on with
            assassinations

SAM   don't allow

JACK   changing our

SAM   do allow

JACK   ok

SAM   so get on with

JACK   cia's health alteration committee

SAM   great

JACK   planning

SAM	Castro, Allende, Ayatollah Khomeini
JACK	Lumumba, Osama, Charles de Gaulle
SAM	Michael Manley
JACK	Ngo Dinh Diem
SAM	but not all the bastards are dead so
JACK	disappeared, thousands and
SAM	all over
JACK	impact
SAM	and what what fucking terror used against us
JACK	not my fault they
SAM	fucking Afghanis turned against us after all we
JACK	training camps and now
SAM	stop them
JACK	I'm
SAM	and Israel, innocent
JACK	body parts
SAM	vile
JACK	but the Israelis killing far more so
SAM	on top of this?
JACK	explosion at the embassy
SAM	fuck fuck do something

JACK	stop shouting at me because
SAM	on my side?
JACK	of course but
SAM	want to go home to your
JACK	maybe I do if you're going to keep
SAM	fuck off then back
JACK	look out we're being
SAM	no no no the towers
JACK	wow
SAM	evil
JACK	ok?
SAM	hate me because I'm so good
JACK	all these terrorists suddenly
SAM	makes everyone love me because it's only the evildoers who hate me, you don't hate me
JACK	no of course
SAM	you hate me
JACK	just sometimes wish you'd
SAM	what? what? you hate me
JACK	but maybe I can't live with you any more

7.

SAM *alone.*

SAM
white double cable whip, iron wreath, beating the soles of the feet, put object in vagina, put object in anus, put turpentine on testicles, play very loud Indonesian music, electric shocks to genitals, tap a dowl through the ear into the brain, throw the prisoner out of the helicopter, show the prisoner another prisoner being thrown out of the helicopter, beating obviously, rape of course, bright light, no sleep, simulate an execution so they think up to the last second they're going to die, play tape of women and children screaming in next room and tell prisoner it's his wife and children, sometimes it is, hang up with hands tied behind back, chop off hands, pins in eyes, insecticide in hood over the head, cut off breasts, pull out heart, slit throat and pull tongue through, sulphuric acid, cut off

Enter JACK.

JACK
hello, I've

SAM
what you

JACK
but I missed you

SAM	same as before
JACK	try and
SAM	what you put me through
JACK	I'm sorry I
SAM	hurt me
JACK	yes I
SAM	take you back I need to know if
JACK	try to
SAM	total commitment or there's no
JACK	I realise
SAM	capable
JACK	can
SAM	promise
JACK	love
SAM	nightmare here
JACK	yes
SAM	not going to be happy, hope you don't
JACK	no I don't expect
SAM	so what you
JACK	can't live
SAM	no you can't, can't
JACK	no I can't

SAM	ok then
JACK	doing?
SAM	need to teach
JACK	yes
SAM	special advisers
JACK	ok
SAM	Greece
JACK	the colonels' Greece, we're right behind
SAM	Operation Phoenix
JACK	Vietnam, operational
SAM	nobody questioned survives
JACK	fortyone thousand
SAM	teaching them in Brazil exactly how much electric shock you can administer without killing
JACK	because sometimes you may not want
SAM	sometimes it's not politic
JACK	and sometimes it just doesnt matter
SAM	El Salvador, Uruguay, Nicaragua, Guatemala,
JACK	delivering the manuals to Panama
SAM	and the thin wire can go in the diplomatic bag to Uruguay
JACK	thin wire?

SAM	against the gum and it increases the shock
JACK	need to be accurate
SAM	precise pain
JACK	for precise effect
SAM	so practice on beggars in a soundproof room
JACK	the US Office of Public Safety
SAM	fighting terror
JACK	put Mitrione in charge of
SAM	humanitarian
JACK	expert in administration of pain
SAM	always leave them some hope, he says
JACK	people who don't need our encouragement because they already
SAM	Afghanistan
JACK	yes the game where the men are on horses and the prisoner
SAM	instead of a goat
JACK	one layer of skin at a time, which must take
SAM	so relatively speaking, Guantanamo
JACK	need results
SAM	need exemption from rules forbidding cruel, inhuman or

JACK	because those rules
SAM	in the present climate
JACK	hoods over their heads or sexual
SAM	because their religion makes them upset by
JACK	menstrual blood
SAM	have to laugh
JACK	but some things we'd rather other people
SAM	boeing 747 rendering prisoners to
JACK	because there's plenty of places where they can
SAM	can't do everything ourselves
JACK	do our best
SAM	you're doing great again
JACK	back with you
SAM	no fun though
JACK	sick today but
SAM	just stick with it and we'll be

8.

JACK	icecaps
SAM	who fucking cares about
JACK	floods
SAM	because we'll all be dead by the time it
JACK	another hurricane moving towards
SAM	natural
JACK	no but it's greater than
SAM	natural disasters
JACK	not coping very
SAM	surprise
JACK	predicted and there is an element of manmade
SAM	stop fucking going on about
JACK	carbon
SAM	junk science.
JACK	report here from the
SAM	rewrites
JACK	'serious threat to health'

SAM   delete

JACK   'growing risk of adverse'

SAM   delete

JACK   'uncertainties'

SAM   insert 'significant and fundamental'

JACK   but

SAM   'urgent action', delete

JACK   oil lobby?

SAM   Committee for a Constructive Tomorrow

JACK   ok

SAM   Advancement of Sound Science Coalition

JACK   a grassroots

SAM   set up by Exxon and Philip Morris to

JACK   ok

SAM   and carbon dioxide in the atmosphere has many beneficial effects on

JACK   hot in here?

SAM   always finding something wrong with

JACK   and you never?

SAM   let's just

JACK   ok

SAM   what? what? you smoking? you gave up, you

JACK   don't care because

SAM   kill yourself

JACK   fucking planet

SAM   kill me, kill me, passive

JACK   junk science

SAM   put it out

JACK   no

SAM   put it out

JACK   what difference

SAM   thank you

JACK   carbon

SAM   can't see it in the air, so

JACK   Kyoto?

SAM   price of electricity in California

JACK   but

SAM   nuclear

JACK   danger

SAM   efficient

JACK   waste

SAM   solution

JACK   Iran?

SAM   Technology Institute will come up with
              new

JACK	by when will they
SAM	if you're so smart
JACK	different
SAM	freedom to
JACK	if
SAM	lose everything we've
JACK	hard to
SAM	things I need
JACK	look out
SAM	what?
JACK	don't know, I thought
SAM	deep breaths and
JACK	don't want to stop flying
SAM	trade in carbon so we can still
JACK	and we'll last longer than
SAM	don't let them in
JACK	no water
SAM	be ok
JACK	catastrophe
SAM	so fucking negative
JACK	frightened
SAM	leave me if you don't

JACK	done that
SAM	stay then and be some
JACK	hopeless
SAM	and try to smile
JACK	dead
SAM	because you have to love me
JACK	can't
SAM	love me love me, you have to love me, you

End.

A Nick Hern Book

Drunk Enough to Say I Love You? first published in Great Britain
as a paperback original in 2006 by Nick Hern Books Limited,
14 Larden Road, London W3 7ST in association with
the Royal Court Theatre, London

Drunk Enough to Say I Love You? copyright © 2006 Caryl Churchill

Caryl Churchill has asserted her right to be identified as
the author of this work

Cover design by Ned Hoste, 2H

Typeset by Country Setting, Kingsdown, Kent CT14 8ES
Printed in Great Britain by Bookmarque, Croydon, Surrey

A CIP catalogue record for this book is available from
the British Library

ISBN-13   978 1 85459 959 9
ISBN-10   1 85459 959 3